PEACE
THE EXHIBITION

Amber Lloydlangston and Kathryn Lyons

CANADIAN WAR MUSEUM
MUSÉE CANADIEN DE LA GUERRE

Library and Archives Canada
Cataloguing in Publication

Lloydlangston, Amber, 1968-
Peace : the exhibition /
Amber Lloydlangston, Kathryn Lyons.

Issued also in French under title:
Paix, l'exposition.
Exhibition catalogue.
Includes bibliographical references.
ISBN 978-0-660-20262-4
Cat. no.: NM23-5/2-2013E

1. Military history--Canada--Exhibitions.
2. Peace--Exhibitions.
3. Canada--Military policy--Exhibitions.
4. Peacekeeping forces, Canadian--Exhibitions.
I. Lyons, Kathryn, 1976-
II. Canadian War Museum
III. Title.

NX650.P4 L96 2013
355'.033071
C2012-980228-X

Published by the
Canadian War Museum
1 Vimy Place
Ottawa, ON K1A 0M8
www.warmuseum.ca

Printed and bound in Canada.
Souvenir Catalogue series, 2
ISSN 2291-6385

CONTENTS

FOREWORD

As much as any other factor in our past, Canada has been shaped by its people's actions for peace. From ancient times to the present day, a variety of issues and events have prompted Canadians to make choices and take action to make peace more possible. These actions have been wide-ranging and sometimes completely opposed to one another: some shouldered arms, and some demonstrated against wars and weapons; some acted as skilled negotiators, and some provided humanitarian aid.

This souvenir catalogue is a companion to the first exhibition to address this complex history. From the longstanding peace of the Six Nations Confederacy, to Canadians' responses to Afghanistan, one fundamental point has applied throughout: no matter what their choice, Canadians have acted with equal conviction and passion, motivated to take action for peace.

Created at the Canadian War Museum, **Peace–The Exhibition** highlights more than 200 items from the collections of both the Canadian War Museum and the Canadian Museum of Civilization. These items, together with an additional 100 borrowed objects, represent a broad range of perspectives, each telling a compelling part of the story of peace in Canada.

As Canada's national museum of military history, the Canadian War Museum's mandate is to explore Canada's responses to conflict in all of its human, national, and international dimensions. We are committed to presenting, in a respectful and thought-provoking manner, the enormous diversity of those responses in new and innovative ways. Canadians will see themselves in **Peace–The Exhibition**. They may also come face to face with people they might never have understood to be working towards the same ultimate goal: peace.

Through this souvenir catalogue and the accompanying exhibition, the Canadian War Museum invites all Canadians to better understand peace—as a force for action and change in our past, and as an ongoing story today.

James Whitham
Director General,
Canadian War Museum,
and Vice-President,
Canadian Museum of
Civilization Corporation

SIX NATIONS CONFEDERACY

"THERE SHALL BE NO MORE FEAR ON EARTH... THERE IS NO ENDING OF PEACE. IT WILL ALWAYS FLOURISH FOR ALL TIME TO COME, AND THIS WILL BECOME THE LAW."

The Peacemaker (the Creator's messenger), as related by Chief Jacob Thomas, September 1992

Long before Europeans arrived in North America, warfare created fear and despair among many First Nations. The Peacemaker and his followers Ayenwatha and Jigonsaseh, the Mother of Nations, persuaded the Haudenosaunee (Iroquois) to unite for peace and security. Their vision became the Great Law of Peace, Power and Righteousness. The Law continues to be a guide to good living, as well as the constitution of the Six Nations Confederacy.

Sharing the Great Law

Elders such as Chief Jacob Thomas, and other teachers, use stories and symbols to share the Great Law. While there is debate about the age of the Confederacy and the Great Law, oral tradition related to its establishment, central figures and symbols has remained constant for centuries. Tradition tells of a Peacemaker who used messengers to gather the warring chiefs under a great white pine tree. There, they were persuaded to “bury their hatchets,” and stop fighting amongst themselves. The tree’s five needles represent strength in unity. Its branches provide shelter, and its roots extend an invitation for others to join.

Tadodaho, Past and Present

Tadodaho, entwined in snakes, symbolizes obstacles to establishing the Great Law. He was the final Chief to stop spreading misfortune, and to agree to use the power of his mind for peace. Tadodaho then took his position as an Onondaga Chief, completing the great Circle of Chiefs that governed the Five Nations. This painting by Tuscarora artist Rick Hill suggests that it can be difficult to follow the Great Law in a modern society: The first Tadodaho (a hereditary title) attempts to corrupt Leon Shenandoah—Tadodaho from 1969 until his death in 1996—by convincing him to ignore the principles of the Great Law.

Five Nations Territorial Belt

This wampum belt celebrates the formation of the Confederacy. From left to right, the squares represent the Kanien´kehaka (Mohawk), O-na´-yote-ka-o-no´ (Oneida), Gwe-u´-gweh-o-no´ (Cayuga) and Nun-da´-wa-o-no´ (Seneca). The centre shape, viewed as either a tree or a heart, signifies the O-nun´-da-ga-o-no´ (Onondaga): the heart of the Confederacy, and the location of the council fire. A sixth nation, the Dus-ga´-o-weh-o-no´ (Tuscarora) joined the Confederacy in the early eighteenth century. The wampum belt itself also represents the Confederacy, appearing on flags and other symbols of identity.

PEACE ACROSS THE BORDER

"...THE WORLD'S LONGEST, UNDEFENDED BORDER... AN EXAMPLE OF NATIONS COEXISTING PEACEFULLY SIDE BY SIDE..."

Stephen Harper,
Canadian Prime Minister,
June 6, 2012

The border between Canada and the United States is a symbol of peace between neighbours. Since the end of the War of 1812, the land and resources in border areas have caused conflict and raised tempers several times, but have never led to war.

The Aroostook War

This is the signature page of the 1842 Webster-Ashburton Treaty, which established the location of the border between Maine and New Brunswick.

Both Maine and New Brunswick claimed the rich timber stands in the Aroostook River valley. A simmering dispute over the border erupted into the 1839 Aroostook War, with both sides sending troops to the region. Soldier-diplomats on the ground negotiated a compromise to prevent violence.

The truce held until Daniel Webster (left) for the Americans and Lord Ashburton (right) for the British negotiated the treaty. Webster and Ashburton were friends, which helped negotiations. Each also represented a government that sought to improve relations with the other. The climate was right for peace.

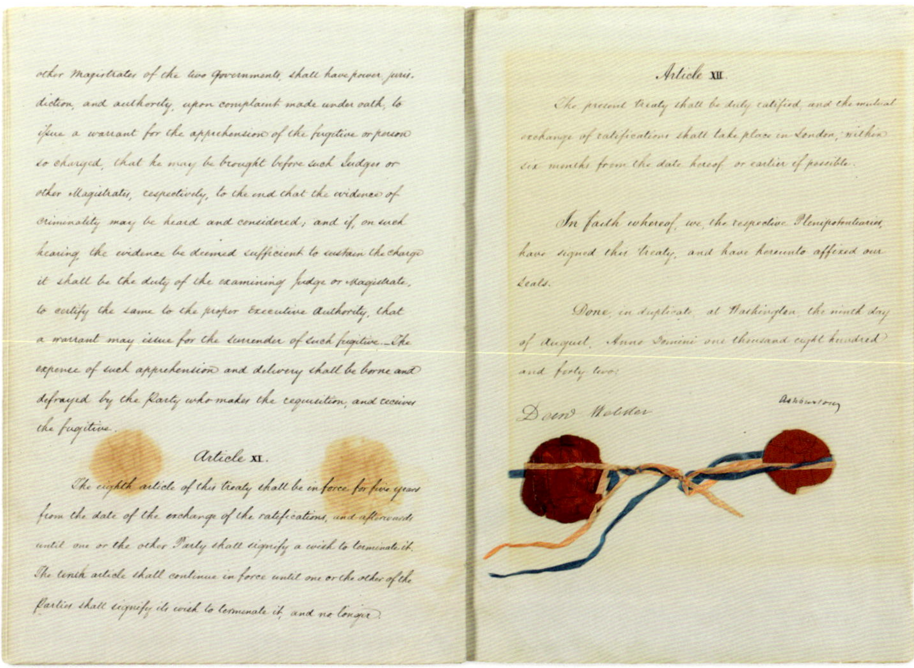

other Magistrates of the two Governments, shall have power, jurisdiction, and authority, upon complaint made under oath, to issue a warrant for the apprehension of the fugitive or person so charged, that he may be brought before such Judges or other Magistrates, respectively, to the end that the evidence of criminality may be heard and considered; and if, on such hearing, the evidence be deemed sufficient to sustain the charge it shall be the duty of the examining Judge or Magistrate, to certify the same to the proper Executive Authority, that a warrant may issue for the surrender of such fugitive.—The expense of such apprehension and delivery shall be borne and defrayed by the Party who makes the requisition, and receives the fugitive.

Article XI.

The eighth article of this treaty shall be in force for five years from the date of the exchange of the ratifications, and afterwards until one or the other Party shall signify a wish to terminate it. The tenth article shall continue in force until one or the other of the Parties shall signify its wish to terminate it, and no longer.

Article XII.

The present treaty shall be duly ratified, and the mutual exchange of ratifications shall take place in London, within six months from the date hereof, or earlier if possible.

In faith whereof, we, the respective Plenipotentiaries, have signed this treaty, and have hereunto affixed our seals.

Done, in duplicate, at Washington, the ninth day of August, Anno Domini one thousand eight hundred and forty two.

Danl Webster   Ashburton

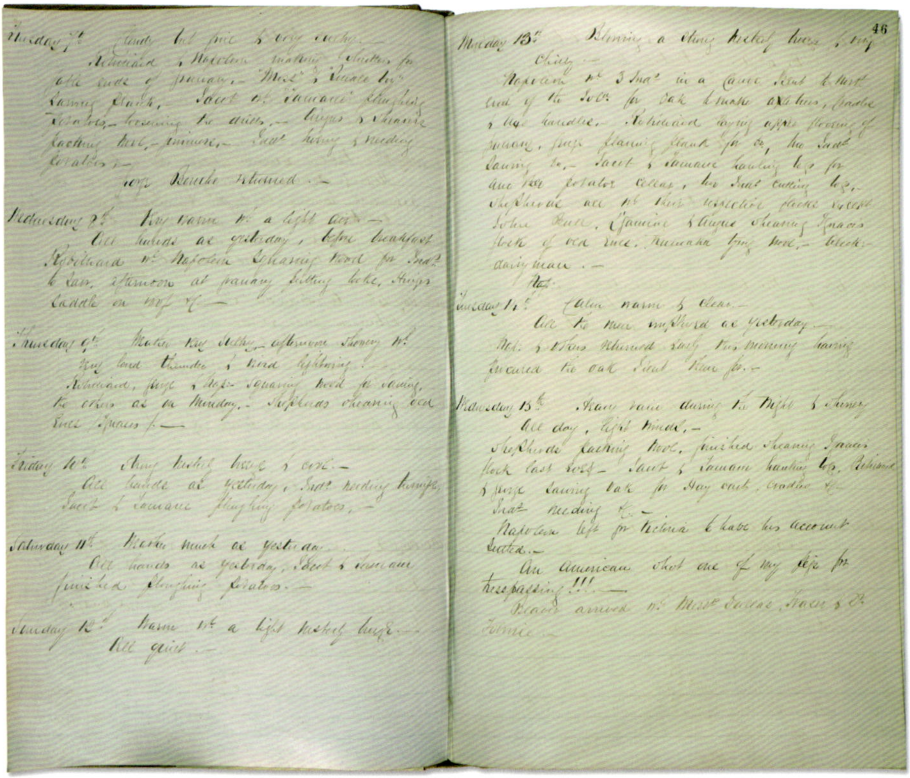

Tuesday 7th Cloudy but fine & very sultry.—
Robillard & Napoleon making shutters for gable ends of granary.— "Moss" & Pierre [illegible] sawing plank.— Scott & Tamanee ploughing potatoes—loosening the drills.— Angus & Shannon packing wool,—[illegible].— Indns hoeing & weeding potatoes.—
Joseph Beuche returned.—

Wednesday 8th Very warm with a light air.—
All hands as yesterday, before breakfast Robillard with Napoleon squaring wood for Indns to saw, afternoon at granary putting [illegible], Angus saddle on [illegible] &c.—

Thursday 9th Weather very sultry, afternoon showery with very loud thunder & vivid lightning!—
Robillard, George & Jos. squaring wood for sawing, the others as on Monday.— Shepherds shearing old Ewes [illegible] &c.—

Friday 10th Strong westerly breeze & cool.—
All hands as yesterday, Indns weeding turnips, Scott & Tamanee ploughing potatoes.—

Saturday 11th Weather much as yesterday.
All hands as yesterday, Scott & Tamanee finished ploughing potatoes.—

Sunday 12th Warm with a light westerly breeze.—
All quiet.—

46

Monday 13th Blowing a strong westerly breeze & very chilly.—
Napoleon with 3 Indns in a canoe went to north end of the Isld. for oak to make axletrees, cradles & axe handles.— Robillard laying upper flooring of granary, George planing plank for do, the Indns sawing do.— Scott & Tamanee hauling logs for new root potatoe cellar, two Indns cutting logs.— Shepherds all at their respective flocks except John Bull, Ganime & Angus shearing Ignace's flock of old ewes. Kanaka tying wool.— Black dairy man.—
Nap.

Tuesday 14th Calm warm & clear.—
All the men employed as yesterday.—
Nap. & others returned early this morning having procured the oak sent them for.—

Wednesday 15th Heavy rain during the night & showery all day, light winds.—
Shepherds packing wool, finished shearing Ignace's flock last Evg.— Scott & Tamanee hauling logs, Robillard & George sawing oak for Hay cart, cradles &c.— Indns weeding &c.—
Napoleon left for Victoria to have his account settled.—
An American shot one of my pigs for trespassing!!!—
Beaver arrived with Messrs Dallas, Fraser & Dr. Tolmie.—

The 1859 Pig War

"An American shot one of my pigs for trespassing!!!" A June 15, 1859 diary entry by Hudson's Bay Company farm manager Charles Griffin includes mention of his pig's shooting death on San Juan Island.

The incident caused an international crisis. Both Britain and the United States had claimed the island, which was rich in resources and militarily significant.

Soon after the pig was shot, 461 American soldiers with 14 cannons faced off against five British warships with 70 guns and 2,140 sailors. Leaders on both sides exercised caution, however, and prevented violence.

American General Winfield Scott and British Columbia governor James Douglas negotiated the joint occupation of the island. This arrangement lasted until arbitration in 1872 gave San Juan Island to the Americans.

YUKON

Yukon Gold

This ring, bearing the word "Yukon," is made of gold mined in the Klondike by American-born prospector Thomas Nixon.

The 1896 Klondike Gold Rush led to a mad influx of people, and focused attention on the unresolved border between Alaska and the Yukon. Canada sought ocean access to the new gold fields through northern Pacific waters. An American land claim barred this access.

In 1903, arbitrators voted to place the border more or less equally between the maximal claims of the two countries. Canadians felt betrayed by Great Britain, because the British arbitrator had sided with the Americans.

TREATY 7

"IN A VERY FEW YEARS, THE BUFFALO WILL PROBABLY BE ALL DESTROYED, AND FOR THIS REASON THE QUEEN WISHES YOU TO ALLOW HER WHITE CHILDREN TO COME AND LIVE ON YOUR LAND AND RAISE CATTLE... SHE WILL ASSIST YOU TO RAISE CATTLE AND GRAIN, AND THUS GIVE YOU THE MEANS OF LIVING WHEN THE BUFFALO ARE NO MORE."

David Laird, Treaty 7 Commissioner and Lieutenant-Governor, Northwest Territories, September 19, 1877

In the 1870s, over-hunting threatened the extinction of bison, and jeopardized the way of life of many of the First Nations in Western Canada. During the same period, the Canadian government wanted the land controlled by First Nations to build the Canadian Pacific Railroad. To satisfy their respective needs, the Canadian government and the Siksika, Kainai, Piikani, Tsuu T'ina and Stoney Nakoda negotiated the terms of a peaceful relationship in Treaty 7.

Crowfoot
ight Secured 1886
Buell

"I WISH ALL MY PEOPLE GOOD, AND TRUST THAT ALL OUR HEARTS WILL INCREASE IN GOODNESS FROM THIS TIME FORWARD. I AM SATISFIED. I WILL SIGN THE TREATY."

Crowfoot, Chief of the Siksika, September 21, 1877

Chief Crowfoot

Crowfoot was a renowned warrior and influential peacemaker, and was a key Siksika representative at the 1877 Treaty 7 negotiations. He recognized that his people's way of life was changing, because the bison were becoming increasingly scarce. He believed that his people needed support to adapt to a new way of life.

He also believed that the Canadian government had agreed to provide such support during negotiations. In exchange, he and other First Nations agreed to share their land peacefully with newcomers. Like many other First Nations, Crowfoot was later disillusioned. The government was slow to implement the written terms of Treaty 7, and disregarded oral promises made during the talks.

Building the Railroad

To promote permanent agricultural settlement, and to solidify a still young and tenuous Confederation, the federal government wanted to construct a railroad. This railroad would bring settlers from the East and supply raw materials to central Canada.

The government could not act, however, until it secured land title from the First Nations who controlled it. As dictated by the *Royal Proclamation of 1763*, this had to be done in an open meeting with all of the affected First Nations. Once Treaty 7 had been accepted, construction of the railroad and of new communities soon followed.

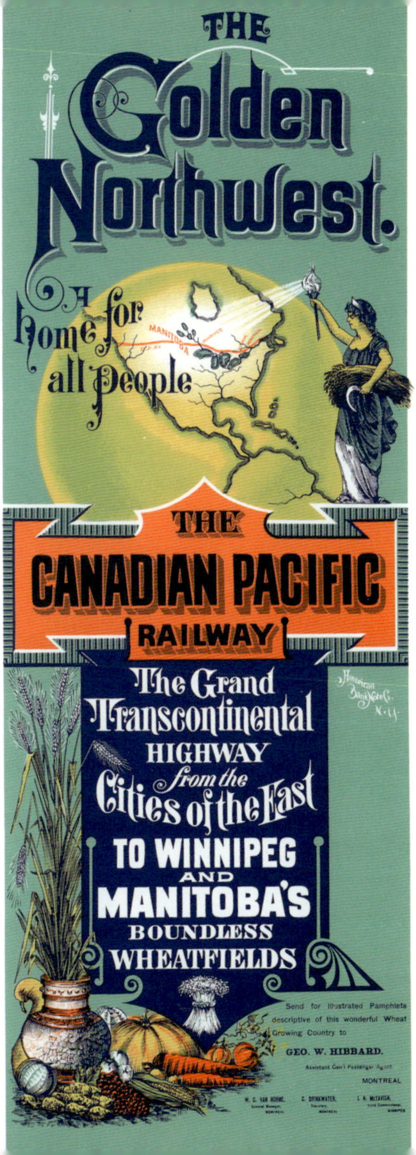
THE
Golden Northwest.
A home for all People
MANITOBA
THE
CANADIAN PACIFIC
RAILWAY
The Grand Transcontinental HIGHWAY from the Cities of the East
TO WINNIPEG
AND
MANITOBA'S
BOUNDLESS
WHEATFIELDS
Send for Illustrated Pamphlets descriptive of this wonderful Wheat Growing Country to
GEO. W. HIBBARD.
MONTREAL
W. C. VAN HORNE.
C. DRINKWATER.
L. A. McTAVISH.

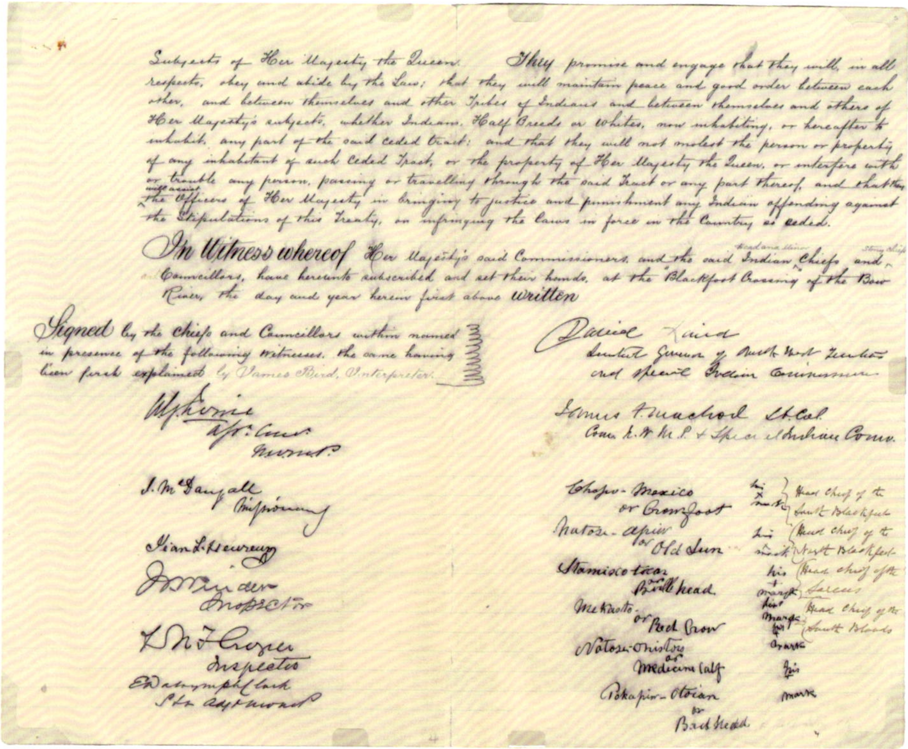

Subjects of Her Majesty the Queen. They promise and engage that they will, in all respects, obey and abide by the Law; that they will maintain peace and good order between each other, and between themselves and other Tribes of Indians and between themselves and others of Her Majesty's subjects, whether Indians, Half Breeds or Whites, now inhabiting, or hereafter to inhabit, any part of the said ceded tract; and that they will not molest the person or property of any inhabitant of such ceded tract, or the property of Her Majesty the Queen, or interfere with or trouble any person, passing or travelling through the said tract or any part thereof, and that they will assist the Officers of Her Majesty in bringing to justice and punishment any Indian offending against the Stipulations of this Treaty, or infringing the laws in force in the Country so ceded.

In Witness whereof Her Majesty's said Commissioners, and the said Indian Head and Minor Chiefs, and Stony Chiefs and Councillors, have hereunto subscribed and set their hands, at the "Blackfoot Crossing" of the Bow River, the day and year herein first above written.

Signed by the Chiefs and Councillors within named in presence of the following witnesses, the same having been first explained by James Bird, Interpreter.

A. G. Irvine
Ast. Comr.
N.W.M.P.

J. McDougall
Missionary

Jean L'Heureux

W. Winder
Inspector

L. N. F. Crozier
Inspector

E. Dalrymple Clark
Lt. & Adjutant

David Laird
Lieutenant Governor of North West Territories and Special Indian Commissioner

James F. Macleod Lt. Col.
Com. N. W. M. P. & Special Indian Comr.

Chapo-Mexico or Crowfoot, his x mark, Head Chief of the South Blackfeet

Matose-Apiw or Old Sun, his x mark, Head Chief of the North Blackfeet

Stamiscotocar or Bull head, his x mark, Head Chief of the Sarcees

Mekasto or Red Crow, his x mark, Head Chief of the South Bloods

Natose-Onistors or Medicine Calf, his x mark

Pokapiw-Otoian or Bad Head, his x mark

Treaty 7

Accepted by government representatives and First Nations chiefs on September 22, 1877, Treaty 7 is a living, relevant document. What had been agreed to during negotiations was disputed from the beginning, however. Canada observed the written terms, while ignoring oral promises and pursuing policies that favoured the assimilation of First Peoples.

Treaty 7 First Nations sought to survive and to push the federal government to respect the terms of the Treaty as they understood them. To demonstrate that the written treaty is problematic, they point to names improperly translated or transcribed phonetically. For example, Crowfoot's name, "Issapo-maksika," is written "Chapo-Mexico." Today, Canada and Treaty 7 First Nations see the treaty as the basis of a relationship of mutual respect and accommodation. Negotiations on other aspects continue.

THE FIRST WORLD WAR

"WELL DARLING ALICE... I LOVE YOU WITH ALL MY HEART AND SOUL, AND I WANT TO MARRY YOU. REMEMBER IT IS FOR THE FREEDOM OF CANADA AND YOU THAT WE ARE FIGHTING."

Canadian Gunner Robert Hale,
Letter to Alice Heath, July 8, 1915

Canadians eagerly chose to fight and support the First World War. Most saw it as a war for justice—one that would restore peace, and later, even one that might "end all wars." The war was costly and long, and strained Canada's resources and unity. At war's end, Canadians considered how best to avoid another war.

"TO HIS COURAGEOUS CONDUCT MUST BE ASCRIBED THE SAVING OF THE LIVES OF MANY OF HIS COMRADES."

***London Gazette*,**
December 14, 1918

One Soldier's Bravery

Private John Francis Young was a stretcher-bearer during the war. Unarmed, his job was to reach, help and remove wounded soldiers from the battlefield. He saved countless lives and was "absolutely fearless." His most conspicuous act of bravery, which earned him the Victoria Cross, involved rushing repeatedly, with no protection from enemy fire, to assist wounded men and transport them to safety.

Young was one of seven Canadians to have been awarded the Victoria Cross during fighting at the Drocourt-Quéant Line on September 2, 1918. Exposed to mustard gas during the battle, Young later contracted tuberculosis. He died in 1929.

"WE HAVE PAID A VERY HEAVY PRICE, BUT I THINK IT IS FINISHED."

Canadian Lieutenant John Adie to his mother Frances on May 3, 1918, six months before his death on November 3, 1918

A Country at War, a Family's Sacrifice

The struggle of the First World War involved almost the entire country, and made enormous demands on the Canadian people. More than 600,000 Canadians served in uniform during the war. In some families—such as the Adie family of St. Catharines, Ontario—all eligible children served.

This banner hung in their family home. Each maple leaf represented a son on active duty overseas. Only one, Robert, survived. John, Archibald and Allan Adie were three of the more than 60,000 Canadians who died in the war.

Lessons from a War for Peace

In the aftermath of the war, Canadians celebrated peace. Munitions manufacturer Goldie & McCulloch featured this sculpture on their Armistice Day parade float on November 11, 1918. The dove on the shell reinforced the idea that the war had been fought for peace.

Canadians wanted to avoid another costly war. Some believed that the war's primary lesson was the need for a large, well-trained military. Others, believing that a more independent Canada should work for peace through the new League of Nations, supported diplomacy more than defence. Still others, including some who saw the war as a great waste, called for Canada's future isolation from Europe's deadly problems and conflicts.

THE SECOND WORLD WAR

"THE FORCES OF EVIL HAVE BEEN LOOSED IN THE WORLD. THAT IS WHY THE PRESENT WAR IS FOR THE ALLIED FORCES A CRUSADE."

William Lyon Mackenzie King,
Canadian Prime Minister,
September 3, 1939

During the 1930s, many Canadians believed that war in Europe was unavoidable. Some hoped to prevent a global conflict by fighting in the Spanish Civil War. But the Second World War (1939–1945) could not be avoided. Tens of thousands of men and women enlisted in Canada's armed forces. Even more women, men and children supported the war effort at home.

"...AND IF I, AN ENRAGED PACIFIST, AM A SOLDIER TODAY, IT'S BECAUSE I HATE WAR. AND TO DESTROY WAR, WE MUST DESTROY THE REGIME THAT IS RESPONSIBLE FOR IT."

Canadian Robert Martineau writing to his friend M. E. Trepannier from Spain, May 20, 1938

The Spanish Civil War

Between 1936 and 1938, almost 1,700 Canadians fought in Spain with the Republicans against Francisco Franco's fascist Nationalists. They chose to do so, even though the Canadian government had declared its neutrality and made it illegal for Canadians to fight for another country. Many believed they were fighting for peace by fighting fascism.

Of the 36 soldiers who signed this souvenir fan in early 1938, 26 were Canadians. By the time the Canadians withdrew from action at the end of 1938, by order of the Spanish government, 13 of those who had signed, including 10 Canadians, had died or gone missing. They were among the more than 700 Canadians who died in the war.

"SOMETHING IS HAPPENING OVER THERE THAT HAS PROFOUNDLY TOUCHED ME, MY CONVICTIONS, AND MY PRINCIPLES."

**Canadian Lieutenant Claude Châtillon,
Royal 22e Régiment, Diary Entry,
January 11, 1942**

Canadians at War

Canada's pre-war army, air force, and navy were tiny. By war's end, more than a million Canadian men and women had left their everyday lives for military service. More than 42,000 died.

Fighting on the ground, in the air and at sea was fierce, taxing the strength of soldiers, aircrew and sailors. Canada's war artists captured some of their experiences. Among the most celebrated was Major Charles Comfort. In this painting, he depicts the typical fighting conditions Canadians endured as they fought bitter street battles against the Germans in Ortona, Italy, in December 1943.

Work Boots

These boots were worn by Mennonite and conscientious objector Elmon Lichti between January 1943 and March 1944. He was among the more than 10,000 pacifist men who chose to serve their country through alternative service. Their beliefs would not allow them to fight or build munitions, but they willingly worked in forestry, built roads and telephone lines, produced fuel, processed food and worked in hospitals.

Lichti was sent to the alternative service camp at Montreal River in northern Ontario, in January 1943, to help build a highway between North Bay and Nipigon. In the spring, he shifted to farming. By November, he was in British Columbia working as a forester.

“WE CANNOT WIN THIS WAR IF WE DON’T FIGHT. WE CANNOT FIGHT THIS WAR IF WE DON’T EAT.”

Ontario Farm Service Force,
***The Ottawa Citizen*, April 6, 1943**

Lending a Hand

Farmerette Inge Oswald wore this sweatshirt as one of the 55,000 children, youth and adults who joined the Ontario Farm Service Force (OFSF) in 1942. The OFSF had been established in 1941 to help family farms engage enough workers to produce the crops required to feed Canadian and British troops and supply local markets.

Farmerettes primarily harvested fruit and vegetables, and worked in canning and packing houses. Oswald did both. She first harvested peaches, until a violent allergic reaction to the peach fuzz forced her to stop. She later worked at a Campbell’s Soup Company factory.

FARM SERVICE FORCE
ONTARIO
WE LEND A HAND

REBUILDING AFTER WAR

"PEACE IS MORE THAN THE ABSENCE OF WAR... PEACE CANNOT EXIST IF THERE IS DISTRESS, HUNGER AND DESPAIR ANYWHERE."

**Lester B. Pearson,
Canadian Ambassador
to the United States,
August 16, 1945**

In the aftermath of the Second World War, Canada helped build a lasting peace. The country provided millions of dollars of food, clothing, medicines and agricultural supplies to the United Nations Relief and Rehabilitation Administration (UNRRA). Between 1947 and 1953, Canada also welcomed European refugees and displaced persons.

Starting Over

These tiny boots tell the story of just three of the 165,000 displaced persons who came to Canada following the war. Polish Jews Leo Beer and Genia Eizenberg survived the Holocaust. Both lost most of their families, including Genia's first husband and child.

They found each other at the Pocking Displaced Persons Camp in Germany, where they married. On May 18, 1947, baby Max was born. Together, they were a new family, but they still needed a home. They found it in Canada in 1949, sponsored by Leo's father, who was already in Canada. The boots arrived with Max. The family treasured them until Max donated them to the Montreal Holocaust Memorial Centre.

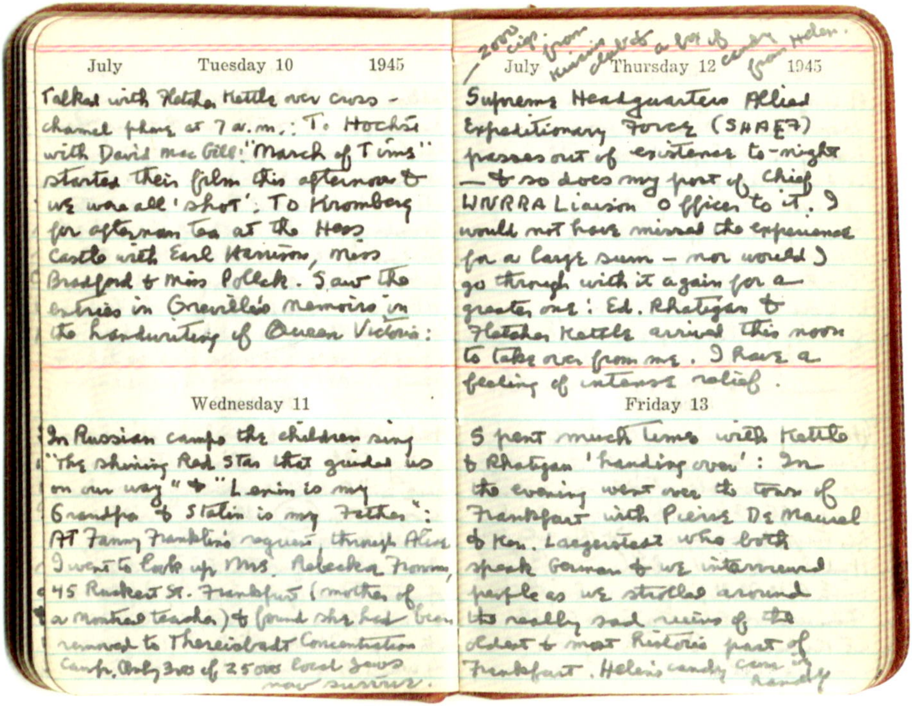

July Tuesday 10 1945

Talked with Fletcher Kettle over cross-channel phone at 7 a.m.: To Hochst with David MacGill: "March of Time" started their film this afternoon & we were all 'shot'. To Kromberg for afternoon tea at the Hess Castle with Earl Harrison, Miss Bradford & Miss Pollak. Saw the entries in Greville's memoirs in the handwriting of Queen Victoria:

Wednesday 11

In Russian camps the children sing "The shining Red Star that guides us on our way" & "Lenin is my Grandpa & Stalin is my Father": At Fanny Franklin's request, through Alice I went to look up Mrs. Rebecka Fromm, 45 Rückert St. Frankfurt (mother of a Montreal teacher) & found she had been removed to Theresienstadt Concentration Camp. Only 300 of 25000 local Jews now survive.

/ 2000 cig. from Kussie [illegible] & a lot of candy from Helen.

July Thursday 12 1945

Supreme Headquarters Allied Expeditionary Force (SHAEF) passes out of existence to-night — & so does my post of Chief UNRRA Liaison Officer to it. I would not have missed the experience for a large sum — nor would I go through with it again for a greater one: Ed. Rhatigan & Fletcher Kettle arrived this noon to take over from me. I have a feeling of intense relief.

Friday 13

Spent much time with Kettle & Rhatigan 'handing over': In the evening went over the town of Frankfurt with Prince De Mérode & Ken. Langenstrass who both speak German & we interviewed people as we strolled around the really sad ruins of the oldest & most historic part of Frankfurt. Helen's candy came in handy.

A Canadian with UNRRA

Canada was the third-largest contributor to UNRRA. In addition to providing goods and money, more than 200 Canadians worked for the agency. Major Alex Edmison, a military lawyer during the war, was one of them. He joined UNRRA in 1945 as its chief spokesperson and director of the care of refugees, displaced persons and concentration camp survivors in France and Germany.

It was a massive task, unparalleled in the size and range of human suffering and need. Edmison documented the horrors of the concentration camps, battled against administrative and military backlogs, and directly helped thousands of people. In this diary, he reflected, "I would not have missed the experience for a large sum—nor would I go through with it again for a greater one."

"...TRULY I FEEL THAT I AM THE MOTHER OF 2,000 CHILDREN."

Canadian Lotta Hitschmanova, 1949

Lotta Hitschmanova

An outspoken opponent of the Nazis, Czechoslovakian Lotta Hitschmanova fled to France in 1942. Sick and malnourished, she received relief there from the Unitarian Service Committee before coming to Canada.

After she regained her health, Hitschmanova worked briefly for UNRRA. It was not enough for her. The sheer extent of the need spurred Hitschmanova to establish her own relief organization in 1945: the Canadian Unitarian Service Committee. She dedicated herself to helping other survivors, particularly children, in France, Czechoslovakia, Austria, Italy and Greece. It was the beginning of her life's work as an international humanitarian.

CANADA

NUCLEAR WEAPONS

"ATOMIC ENERGY CAN BE A FORCE FOR GOOD—A FORCE TO HELP MAINTAIN PEACE THROUGH FEAR OF ITS ALMOST INCOMPREHENSIBLE POWER."

Douglas Harkness, Canadian Minister of National Defence, November 1, 1961

What did peace mean in a nuclear-armed world? Most Canadians believed that nuclear weapons were necessary to preserve peace and security. Canada was a member of the nuclear-armed Western alliance and, for a time, maintained nuclear weapons on its soil. Canada also worked internationally to manage nuclear arsenals. Other Canadians supported more immediate action against nuclear weapons. These ranged from restrictions on testing to complete and unilateral disarmament.

FROM SEA TO SEA...
D'UN OCEAN À L'AUTRE...
...OUR
NUCLEAR
SAFETY
PROGRAM
is your PROTECTION!
...NOTRE
PROGRAMME
DE SÉCURITÉ
NUCLÉAIRE
vous PROTÈGE!
DNW POSTER 1-79

Safeguarding the West

Canada has played an integral role in the nuclear defence of the West since the late 1940s, as a member of nuclear-armed alliances. Canadian military personnel planned ways in which nuclear weapons could be used, and trained to implement these plans.

Canada also fielded four nuclear weapons systems. One of them was the nuclear-armed genie rocket carried by CF-101 Voodoos, like the ones pictured on this poster. The Voodoos were intended to intercept incoming Soviet bombers. They never fired nuclear weapons.

All four systems were implemented after Lester B. Pearson won the 1963 federal election. That election had given Canadians a choice: John Diefenbaker and his seeming reluctance to accept nuclear weapons, or Lester B. Pearson, and his commitment to them.

Greenpeace

This flag, featuring the peace sign and ecology symbol, flew on the first *Greenpeace* ship in 1971. The Greenpeace group hoped to block Americans from conducting an underground nuclear test on Amchitka Island, off the coast of Alaska.

They set sail from Vancouver, British Columbia, on September 15 to begin "the Greenpeacing of America." Although the ship did not stop the test, the voyage captured widespread public attention.

Canadian opposition to nuclear weapons grew through the 1980s. Since 1984, Canada's military has not had nuclear weapons. Canada continues to cooperate with the United States and its nuclear weapons program, however, and is a member of nuclear-armed alliances.

GREENPEAC

"TO REMEMBER HIROSHIMA IS TO COMMIT ONESELF TO PEACE."

Canadian Setsuko Thurlow,
August 11, 2011

Setsuko Thurlow

This clock is from Hiroshima, Japan. Setsuko Thurlow retrieved it from the rubble of her home, after the city was devastated by an atomic blast in 1945. She was 13 years old. After studying in the United States and marrying a Canadian, she moved to Toronto in 1955.

She treasured the clock for more than 60 years as a symbol of her commitment to work for nuclear disarmament. She helped establish the Peace Garden in Toronto's Nathan Phillips Square, and served with a number of peace organizations. In 2007, she was awarded the Order of Canada.

SUEZ CRISIS

"THE TIME HAS COME FOR THE UN, NOT ONLY TO BRING ABOUT A CEASE-FIRE, BUT TO MOVE IN AND POLICE THE CEASE-FIRE AND MAKE ARRANGEMENTS FOR A POLITICAL SETTLEMENT."

**Lester B. Pearson,
Canadian Secretary of
State for External Affairs,
November 3, 1956**

The 1956 Suez Crisis—involving Israel as well as Canada's traditional allies, the United Kingdom and France—threatened to escalate the Cold War. At the United Nations (UN), Canadian Secretary of State Lester B. Pearson proposed an innovative solution: the intervention of an armed, impartial United Nations peacekeeping force. The first United Nations Emergency Force (UNEF I) preserved peace in the region for 10 years.

Pearson's Nobel Prize

Canadian Secretary of State Lester B. Pearson won the Nobel Peace Prize for his role in creating the first United Nations Emergency Force in 1956. Pearson had worked intensely, both at home and at the UN, to negotiate a solution to the crisis. The result—an unarmed, impartial, international military presence—ended the Suez Crisis.

Pearson's actions in the United Nations, which had resolved the crisis, were not uniformly celebrated by Canadians, however. While many were proud, others criticized Pearson and the Liberals for failing to support Canada's traditional allies.

"NEVER BEFORE HAVE SOLDIERS (WHOSE PRIMARY VOCATION IS FIGHTING) BEEN CALLED TOGETHER... FOR SO HONOURABLE A TASK."

Canadian Major
Robin Benjamin Mallory,
1966

General E.L.M. Burns

Burns was in the Middle East commanding a UN mission when UNEF I was established. He was appointed its first commanding officer, due to the respect he had gained among local leaders.

Burns also saved Canada's broader participation in the mission. Canada had wanted to send its Queen's Own Rifles. Egypt's Gamal Abdel Nasser argued that they were too British, and rejected them. Burns negotiated with both sides, and achieved the compromise that Canada would send air transport, support and logistical units.

Burns was commander of UNEF I until December 1959, and later became Canada's representative in nuclear disarmament talks.

Blue Beret

Military personnel from 10 different countries, including Canada, began to arrive in the Middle East in mid-November 1956. They wore the new UN blue berets and helmets. By March 1957, Canada had contributed more than 1,000 of the over 6,000 personnel serving with UNEF I.

The Royal Canadian Air Force transported people and supplies. Canada also formed four new units to provide vital support in the areas of logistics, transport and reconnaissance. With their international counterparts, Canadians staffed observations posts, conducted mobile patrols and carried out air surveillance of the frontier region. For 10 years, they ensured that fighting did not resume.

UN
EMERGENCY FORCE

VIETNAM

"...GIVE PEACE A CHANCE."

John Lennon,
Montréal, Quebec,
June 2, 1969

Canada did not fight in the Vietnam War (1955–1975). Canadians were still deeply involved, however, through government policies and decisions, and a range of individual and group actions—both for and against.

BARIA LONG KHANH

Canada's Official Presence

Captain Fletcher Thomson was one of a small number of Canadian military personnel to serve on two unsuccessful international commissions aimed at containing the conflict in Vietnam.

The same Cold War divisions between Communists and non-Communists that had been at play during the war crippled both commissions. Commission members were not combatants, but there was still danger. Thomson was taken captive by the Viet Cong, a Communist guerilla force. He kept the shirt they gave him. "Baria Long Khanh" is a South Vietnamese province and "28 Jun to 15 Jul 73" are the dates of his captivity. Canada withdrew all its personnel by the end of July 1973.

"...WE SAW THAT WE WOULDN'T HAVE A CHANCE TO GET THE FREEDOM TO GIVE OUR CHILDREN A BETTER FUTURE."

Canadian Thu Vu, former Vietnamese refugee, September 17, 2012

Refugees

After the Communist North won the war, more than one million people fled Vietnam, Laos and Cambodia. Many found temporary refuge in camps in Hong Kong, Thailand and Malaysia. Among them were Thu Vu, her husband and their young son. When they first arrived at the Pulau Bidong refugee camp in Malaysia in April 1980, all they had left were these clothes: Vu's sweater, her husband's ragged shirt and their son's pyjamas. They had been robbed twice during their voyage—including once by pirates, who doused all the women with diesel fuel. The family came to Canada in 1980, sponsored by Vu's brother. By then, Canada had accepted 60,000 of these refugees.

MALAYSIAN
RED CRESCENT
SOCIETY

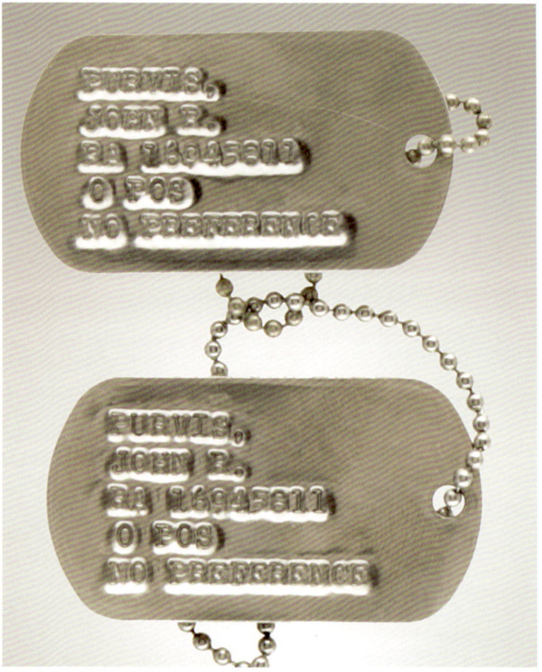
PURVIS,
JOHN P.
O POS
NO PREFERENCE
PURVIS,
JOHN P.
O POS
NO PREFERENCE

An Airborne Ranger

Winnipegger Rob Purvis received these dog tags when he joined the United States military in 1968. He was one of the as many as 30,000 to 40,000 Canadians who enlisted with the American military and fought in Vietnam, even though it was illegal to do so. Like Purvis, some sought adventure. Others believed that communism was a dangerous threat to world peace, and fought to stop its expansion. Purvis served one 12-month tour in Vietnam.
121 Canadians who served with the U.S. military are known to have died in Vietnam.

Claire Culhane, Anti-Vietnam War Protester

After six months working in a South Vietnamese hospital, 51 year-old Claire Culhane returned to Canada opposed to the war and what she saw as Canada's role in it.

For a year, she tried to convince Canada to condemn the war, then established "Camp Enough." For three weeks in December 1969 and January 1970, from her tent near Parliament Hill, she distributed leaflets and tried to meet with Prime Minister Pierre Trudeau. Thousands of Canadians organized and participated in other forms of protest against the war.

ENOUGH
VILLAGE
WE SAY ENOUGH KILLING IN VIETNAM
WE SAY ENOUGH CANADIAN SUPPORT
FOR THIS ENDLESS WAR....
COME AND TALK TO US–
CLARE CULHANE
MICHAEL RUBBO

HAITI

"NOW, MORE THAN EVER, IT IS TIME FOR US TO SHOW OUR SOLIDARITY WITH THE MOST VULNERABLE PEOPLE IN THE AMERICAS: OUR BROTHERS AND SISTERS IN HAITI, WHOSE COURAGE IS ONCE AGAIN BEING SO HARSHLY TESTED."

Michaëlle Jean,
Governor General of Canada,
January 13, 2010

From the 1950s onwards, as Haitians immigrated to Canada and Canadians visited Haiti, Canadians learned of the dire conditions endured by many Haitians. This prompted Canada and Canadians to become increasingly involved in Haiti. Both before and after the devastating earthquake on January 12, 2010, Canada and Canadians provided humanitarian aid, promoted political stability and respect for human rights, and helped to reduce violence in Haiti.

Canadian Forces in Haiti

Haitian-born Canadian Major Marc-Bernard Philippe painted this scene depicting interactions between Haitians and Canadians serving with the UN. The Creole text says "Thank you, Canada, for OP Pivot." OP Pivot was Canada's name for its mission to Haiti from March 1995 to March 1996, as part of a larger UN mission.

Canada has participated in a series of UN missions to Haiti, which have aimed to reduce violence, restore stability and provide humanitarian assistance. Haiti continues to be a priority for the Canadian government at the United Nations.

philippe

The Earthquake

On January 12, 2010, a 7.3-magnitude earthquake struck Haiti near Port-au-Prince.

It killed over 222,000 people—including 58 Canadians—injured more than 300,000, and left 2.3 million homeless. The destruction of infrastructure, combined with a loss of personnel, restricted Haiti's ability to help its people.

The response of Canada and Canadians to the disaster was massive. The Canadian Forces deployed to provide immediate help. Canadian public servants were sent to provide expertise. Canadian NGOs mobilized to provide humanitarian assistance. Ordinary Canadians gave millions of dollars.

Thank you for all your support and generosity.
Sat
2012
December

"DESPITE BEING 4,000 MILES AWAY, AND THE DIFFERENCE IN LANGUAGE AND CULTURE, OUR LITTLE COMMUNITY HAS DONE AN INCREDIBLE JOB."

Bob Beckett, Fire Chief,
Langford, British Columbia,
May 17, 2011

Rebuilding Children's Lives

The residents of the Baby Jesus of Prague Orphanage in Port-au-Prince survived the earthquake; their home did not.

RCMP Corporal Christine Briand lived through the earthquake herself, and spearheaded efforts to rebuild the orphanage.

She discovered that the residents of Langford, British Columbia were looking for a way to help. By buying calendars like this—among other activities—the community raised $250,000. In 2012, the new orphanage, built to post-disaster standards, opened with proud and happy members of Langford's "Team Haiti Children" present.

Although her posting to Haiti has ended, Briand continues to visit the children, and treasures the notes and art she receives.

LANDMINES

"ANTI-PERSONNEL LANDMINES SOWN AT RANDOM WITH NO REGARD FOR THE LAWS OF WAR HAVE BECOME A SCOURGE OF HUMANITY. CANADA HAS NOT BEEN PART OF THE PROBLEM, BUT WE WILL CERTAINLY BE PART OF THE SOLUTION."

**David Collenette,
Canadian Minister
of National Defence,
January 17, 1996**

During the Cold War, some armies, including Canada's, used landmines as an effective defence strategy, removing them when they left. Other armies and guerilla groups, however, planted and left behind millions of landmines. Landmines killed and maimed civilians and slowed post-war rebuilding in many countries. Decision-makers, activist organizations and private citizens united in the 1990s in a campaign to outlaw anti-personnel mines. Their joint action was historic, unorthodox and unprecedented.

Canadian Connection

Even before the landmine ban, the Canadian military was concerned with landmines. Their responsible use was a part of Canadian defence planning, and military personnel were involved in landmine-awareness campaigns and demining around the world.

In 1994, Master Corporal Mark Isfeld was clearing up to 60 landmines per day in Croatia. During the early 1990s, millions of landmines were laid by both sides in the conflict in that region. He was killed on June 21, 1994, when the vehicle behind which he was walking triggered two landmines.

The Ottawa Process

On December 3, 1997, Foreign Affairs Minister Lloyd Axworthy (*seated*) signed the Mine Ban Treaty for Canada. This concluded the Ottawa Process, which began in October 1996, when Axworthy challenged countries to meet in Ottawa a year later to sign an anti-personnel landmine ban agreement.

Politicians, diplomats and members of non-governmental organizations (NGOs) drafted the Treaty and worked for its acceptance. By December 1997, 122 countries had agreed to sign it.

Other countries had a variety of reasons not to sign. These included the fact that landmines protected borders, and that the treaty did not cover other armed groups.

Jody Williams (*far left*), and the International Campaign to Ban Landmines—the umbrella organization that had mobilized public support and action for the ban—were awarded the Nobel Peace Prize in 1997.

Lasting Legacy

This prosthetic leg was made at the Tajikistan Orthopedic Centre, which operates with the help of the Canadian Red Cross. The Centre has provided free artificial limbs to more than 3,000 people injured by landmines and other unexploded ordnance left over from the 1992–1996 civil war.

One legacy of the landmine ban is a dramatic reduction in the production, trade and use of landmines. Mined lands have been reclaimed. Millions of dollars have been donated to help survivors.

Canada continues to help communities affected by landmines through education and aid money.

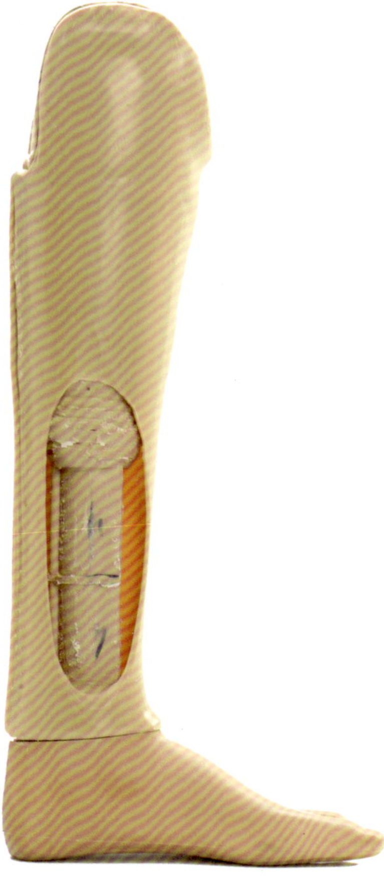

AFGHANISTAN

"THAT'S WHAT WE'RE HERE TO DO: TO HELP."

**Canadian Lieutenant
Aaron Corey,
October 12, 2008**

For over ten years, Canada has intervened in Afghanistan. From 2001 to 2011, Canada was part of a North Atlantic Treaty Organization (NATO) combat mission there. In July 2011, Canada ended its combat commitment. A Canadian Forces mission to train Afghan National Security Forces is scheduled to end in 2014. The Canadian government and Canadian NGOs have also been involved in supporting the Afghan government and providing development support.

"YOU'RE FIRING AT THE ENEMY IN ONE DIRECTION, YOU'RE HANDING OUT BLANKETS AND FOOD TO LOCALS, YOU'RE CARING FOR THE WOUNDED, WHEN THE ORIGINAL MISSION WAS TO COME AND HAVE A *SHURA* [MEETING]."

Canadian Captain Jay Adair, 2006

Patrolling in Afghanistan

More than 30,000 Canadian Forces personnel have served in Afghanistan. A defining experience for many was patrolling. During regular patrols, soldiers fought insurgents and searched for IEDs (improvised explosive devices) or weapons. They also aimed to build trust with local Afghans through meetings and aid. Hundreds of Canadian military personnel have been wounded, and 158 were killed.

ELIZABETH II DEI GRATIA REGINA
CANADA

Bushra Saeed-Khan

Canadian civilian police, public servants and members of NGOs have also aimed to improve conditions in Afghanistan. They have assisted with elections and other government functions, supported health and education, and provided funding to Afghans.

This Sacrifice Medal and General Service Medal belong to Bushra Saeed-Khan. Working for the Canadian government, Saeed-Khan addressed border and drug issues, and worked to build links with Afghans in Kandahar. On December 30, 2009, she was severely injured when her convoy hit an IED. Four soldiers and one journalist were killed. Following a lengthy recovery, Saeed-Kahn returned to work in Ottawa.

"I HAVE SEEN TERRORIST ATTACKS, I HAVE SEEN MY MOTHER GET BEATEN, I HAVE SEEN MY SIBLINGS CRYING FOR A PIECE OF BREAD; BUT NOW, WHILE PREPARING FOR PEACE DAY, I CAN REALLY IMAGINE PEACE INSIDE ME, WHICH IS HARD TO EXPLAIN WITH WORDS."

Afghan youth,
Peace Day, Skateistan,
September 2012

A Helping Hand

Young Afghans attending Skateistan made these puppets. A co-educational school, Skateistan was founded locally in Kabul in 2007, and is now an international charitable organization. Canadian volunteers like Rhianon Bader help run the school.

The school uses skateboarding to attract boys and girls of all backgrounds—especially those working on the streets. Once hooked by skateboarding, the children attend classes that teach leadership skills and civic responsibility.

Divided Opinion

From the beginning, Canadians have debated the scale and scope of Canada's involvement in Afghanistan. Most supported Canada's initial decision to join NATO in the fight against al-Qaida and Taliban forces, believing that military intervention was necessary to restore peace. Support for Canada's current training mission in the country continues.

Others opposed Canada's military intervention, arguing that peace could, and should, be achieved by other means.

Many Canadians, of varying opinions, have continued to support humanitarian and development work in the country.

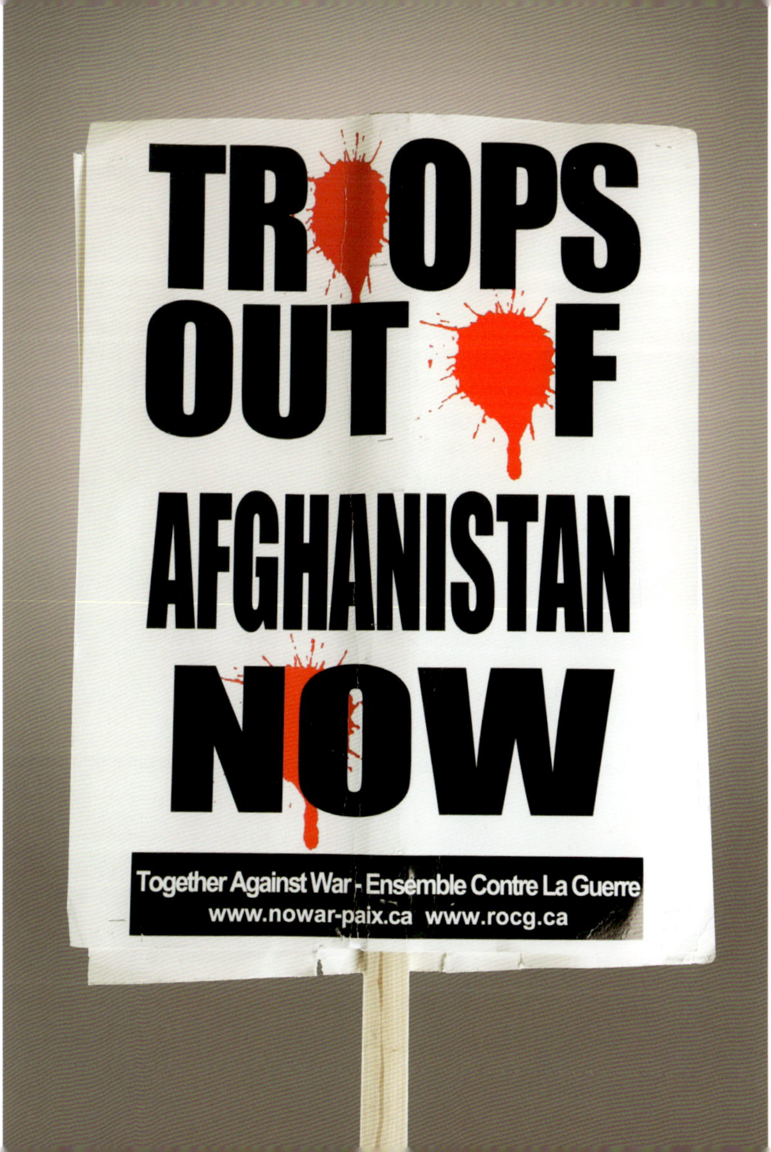
TROOPS
OUT OF
AFGHANISTAN
NOW
Together Against War - Ensemble Contre La Guerre
www.nowar-paix.ca www.rocg.ca

PHOTO CREDITS

p. 7 Jack Haley/Messenger Post Media
p. 8 Courtesy of Yvonne Thomas
p. 11 Woodland Cultural Centre, *Tadodaho, Past and Present*, Rick Hill—Photo: William Kent
p. 12 © Canadian War Museum, CWM 20110089-001—Photo: William Kent
p. 15 The Canadian Press
p. 17 National Archives and Records Administration, Washington, D.C., Record Group 11: General Records of the United States Government, 1778–2006
p. 18 Hudson's Bay Company Archives, Archives of Manitoba, HBCA B.15-a-2
p. 20 © Canadian Museum of Civilization, 983.85.4—Photo: William Kent
p. 23 Glenbow Archives NA-13-1
p. 24 O.B. Buell, Library and Archives Canada, C-001871
p. 27 Canadian Pacific Archives, A6418
p. 28 Library and Archives Canada, *Western Treaty no. 7*, 1877, e002995413—e002995422
p. 31 © Canadian War Museum, CWM 19920085-294—Canadian War Records Office
p. 32 © Canadian War Museum, CWM 20110065-001—Photo: William Kent
p. 35 © Canadian War Museum, CWM 20070073-001—Photo: William Kent
p. 36 © Canadian Museum of Civilization, 77-460—Photo: William Kent
p. 39 Library and Archives Canada, PA-132790
p. 40 © Canadian War Museum, CWM 20130022-002—Photo: William Kent
p. 43 © Canadian War Museum, *Via Dolorosa, Ortona*, Charles Comfort, Beaverbrook Collection of War Art, CWM 19710261-2308—Photo: William Kent
p. 44-45 Mennonite Heritage Centre—Photo: William Kent
p. 47 © Canadian War Museum, CWM 20120014-002—Photo: William Kent
p. 49 City of Vancouver Archives, CVA 586-3976—Photo: Don Coltman, Steffens Colmer
p. 51 Montreal Holocaust Memorial Centre—Photo: William Kent
p. 52 Queen's University Archives, J.A. Edmison fonds, Locator #2501, Box 6, *Overseas Diaries*, 1941–1946
p. 55 Library and Archives Canada, Canadian Unitarian Service Committee, PA-165329

p. 57 Photograph Courtesy of National Nuclear Security Administration Nevada Site Office
p. 58 © Canadian War Museum, CWM 19800103-078—Photo: William Kent
p. 61 City of Vancouver Archives, Greenpeace Foundation Fonds, AM925, S4, Bay 220-B—Photo: William Kent
p. 62 © Canadian War Museum, CWM 20100041-001—Photo: William Kent
p. 65 Department of National Defence
p. 67 Duncan Cameron, National Archives of Canada, C-094168
p. 68 © Canadian War Museum, *E. L .M. Burns*, Lilias Torrance Newton, Beaverbrook Collection of War Art, CWM 19730315-001—Photo: William Kent
p. 71 © Canadian War Museum, CWM 19790218-003—Photo: William Kent
p. 73 York University Libraries, Clara Thomas Archives & Special Collections, Toronto Telegram fonds, ASC00726
p. 74 © Canadian War Museum, CWM 19950113-001—Photo: William Kent
p. 77 Thu Vu—Photo: William Kent
p. 78 Rob Purvis—Photo: William Kent
p. 81 The William Ready Division of Archives and Research Collections, McMaster University Library
p. 83 Department of National Defence
p. 85 © Canadian War Museum, *Peacekeepers*, Marc Bernard Philippe, 1995, Beaverbrook Collection of War Art, CWM 19970043-001—Photo: William Kent
p. 86-87 GlobalMedic
p. 88 City of Langford and Christine Briand—Photo: William Kent
p. 91 Land Mine Victims Cambodia by Michael S. Lewis, MD. Reproduced courtesy of the American Academy of Orthopaedic Surgeons' eMotion Pictures: *An Exhibition of Orthopaedics in Art*
p. 93 Courtesy of Marcus Isfeld
p. 94 The Canadian Press
p. 97 Canadian Red Cross—Photo: William Kent
p. 99 Department of National Defence
p. 100 Department of National Defence
p. 102 Bushra Saeed-Khan—Photo: William Kent
p. 103 Bushra Saeed-Khan—Photo: William Kent
p. 104 Skateistan—Photo: William Kent
p. 107 © Canadian War Museum, CWM 20070027-004—Photo: William Kent